TRAVEL WITH THE GREAT EXPLORERS

Explore with

Giovanni da Verrazzano

Cynthia O'Brien

Crabtree Publishing Company
www.crabtreebooks.com

Crabtree Publishing Company

www.crabtreebooks.com

Author: Cynthia O'Brien

Managing Editor: Tim Cooke

Designer: Lynne Lennon

Picture Manager: Sophie Mortimer

Design Manager: Keith Davis

Editorial Director: Lindsey Lowe

Children's Publisher: Anne O'Daly

Crabtree Editorial Director: Kathy Middleton

Crabtree Editor: Petrice Custance

Proofreader: Angela Kaelberer

**Production coordinator
and prepress technician:** Tammy McGarr

Print coordinator: Margaret Amy Salter

Written and produced for Crabtree Publishing Company
by Brown Bear Books

Photographs:
Front Cover: **Public Domain:** Mauro Guanandi cr; **Shutterstock:** S. Bonaime br, C. Mircea tr; **Topfoto:** Granger Collection main.

Interior: **Alamy:** Gennadly Guchek 15br, ImageBroker 27r, National Geographic Creative 21r, North Wind Picture Archives 13, 25t; **istockphoto:** Denis Tangney Jr 7b; **Library of Congress:** 19br; **Musée du Louvre:** 10; **NARA:** 19t; **NASA:** 15l; **Public Domain:** 11t, 24-25b, Christie's New York 14r, Mauro Guanandi 25br, Jim Henderson 16, Sebastiao Lopes/Charles R. Boxer 12b, Popular Science Monthly 28, Andre Thevet/Internet Archive 11br; **Shutterstock:** 29b, S. Bonaime 14bl, Leoks 22t, Thomas E. Malloy 7t, Mark Van Dyke Photography 6bl, Ann Pics 20, J. Smith 22b, Sui-Lyn 20-21b, Wollertz 17tl, Andrey Yurlov 26; **Thinkstock:** Baratroli 4-5b, Kyle Bedell 5r, Brian Delft/Dorling Kindersley 12t, istockphoto 17br, John North 17cr, Claudia Prommegger 23bl, Gary Tog 6tr; **Topfoto:** ClassicStock 18, Granger Collection 4, 23tr, 29t, World History Archive 27bl.
All other artwork and maps, **Brown Bear Books Ltd**.

Brown Bear Books has made every attempt to contact the copyright holder. If you have any information please contact licensing@brownbearbooks.co.uk

---

Library and Archives Canada Cataloguing in Publication

CIP Available at the Library and Archives Canada

Library of Congress Cataloging-in-Publication Data

Names: O'Brien, Cynthia (Cynthia J.), author.
Title: Explore with Giovanni da Verrazzano / Cynthia O'Brien.
Description: New York, NY : Crabtree Publishing Company, 2018. |
    Series: Travel with the great explorers | Includes index.
Identifiers: LCCN 2017028418 (print) | LCCN 2017030905 (ebook) |
    ISBN 9781427178121 (Electronic HTML) |
    ISBN 9780778739227 (reinforced library binding : alk. paper) |
    ISBN 9780778739289 (pbk. : alk. paper)
Subjects: LCSH: Verrazzano, Giovanni da, 1485-1528--Juvenile literature. |
    America--Discovery and exploration--French--Juvenile literature. |
    Explorers--America--Biography--Juvenile literature. |
    Explorers--France--Biography--Juvenile literature.
Classification: LCC E133.V5 (ebook) | LCC E133.V5 O27 2018 (print) |
    DDC 910.92 [B] --dc23
LC record available at https://lccn.loc.gov/2017028418

Crabtree Publishing Company

www.crabtreebooks.com   1-800-387-7650

Printed in Canada/092017/PB20170719

Published in Canada
Crabtree Publishing
616 Welland Ave.
St. Catharines, ON
L2M 5V6

Published in the United States
Crabtree Publishing
PMB 59051
350 Fifth Avenue, 59th Floor
New York, New York 10118

Published in the United Kingdom
Crabtree Publishing
Maritme House
Basin Road North, Hove
BN41 1WR

Published in Australia
Crabtree Publishing
3 Charles Street
Coburg North
VIC, 3058

CONTENTS

Meet the Boss

Did you know ?

No one knows how Verrazzano spelled his name. In Latin records, it appears as Verazanus. Most now spell it as "Verrazzano," but sometimes it only has one "z," as on the Verrazano Bridge in New York.

Mystery surrounds the early life of the Italian explorer Giovanni da Verrazzano. Later, his adventures led him to the French court and on historic voyages across the Atlantic Ocean to the "New World" of the Americas.

UNCERTAIN IDENTITY

+ Lack of records

There are no primary sources about Giovanni da Verrazzano's early life. There is not even a record of his birth, so historians are not sure when and where Verrazzano was born. Although Verrazzano spent much of his life in France, he referred to himself as a Florentine, meaning he came from Florence in what is now Italy. Most scholars believe he was probably born around 1485 in Val di Greve, near Florence.

CHILD OF THE RENAISSANCE

☛ **Florentine childhood**

☛ **Growing up in a center of culture**

Verrazzano's birthplace, Florence (right), was a center of the Renaissance, a time of great advances in art, science, and philosophy. A new way of thinking began in Florence in the 1300s and spread across Europe. People challenged old ways of thinking and put a new emphasis on education and exploration. As the son of wealthy traders, Verrazzano was educated in this new way.

EARLY TRAVELS

- Young Verrazzano leaves Florence
- Good at languages

As a young man, it seems likely that Verrazzano did some traveling. He may have picked up some sailing skills on ships in the Mediterranean Sea. Some **circumstantial** evidence suggests he visited Syria and Egypt, and may have lived for a time in Cairo. Verrazzano may have been working as a merchant during this time. European traders regularly traveled for business. Verrazzano's early travels may have inspired him to explore farther.

My Explorer Journal

★ Imagine you are a young Verrazzano, and you hear about a "new world" in the Americas. What reasons can you think of to explore the new land? And what reasons are there to stay home?

THE NEW WORLD

+ Sailing for France

In the late 1400s, explorers such as John Cabot and Christopher Columbus crossed the Atlantic Ocean. Their tales of the New World excited European rulers eager to expand their territory and find new trade routes. By 1506, Verrazzano was living in Dieppe, France. Two years later, he took a place on *La Pensée*, a ship captained by Thomas Aubert. Aubert sailed to what is now Canada to fish and to explore. For Verrazzano, it was a first taste of real adventure.

REVEALING LETTER

★ Report to the King

The only record of Verrazzano's voyages is a letter the explorer wrote to King Francis I in July 1524. The letter describes exploring the northeastern shore of North America (above). Early historians were not sure that Verrazzano wrote the letter, but today most people believe he did write it. It contains some clues about Verrazzano. For example, his use of language and math shows that he was well educated.

Where Are We Heading?

Verrazzano explored the eastern coast of North America. He brought Europeans information about the land and people they had never known before.

A NEW LAND

- La Dauphine makes landfall
- Low-lying cape

After crossing the Atlantic Ocean on *La Dauphine*, Verrazzano spotted land in March 1524. He sailed south and then north again to find a place to land. He anchored near present-day Cape Fear, a **headland** in North Carolina (right). Cape Fear is a **tidewater** area where the Cape Fear River flows into the sea. In his famous letter to the French king, Verrazzano noted, "There appeared a new land which had never been seen before by any man."

ROUTE TO CHINA?

+ Verrazzano gazes on a new "sea"

North of Cape Fear, Verrazzano passed the Outer Banks, a series of sand islands (left). Beyond the islands, Verrazzano could see more water. He concluded that he had found a sea that led to the Pacific Ocean, noting, "This is doubtless the one which goes around the tip of India, China, and Cathay." In fact, he had found Pamlico **Sound**, a huge coastal bay. In 1585, the English founded their first American colony at Roanoke, on the Outer Banks.

A GREAT LAKE

★ **Investigating inland**

★ **Missed opportunity**

As the expedition headed north, Verrazzano passed what is now Chesapeake Bay and Delaware Bay. Farther north, he discovered an opening between Staten Island and Long Island. Today, this passage is called the Verrazano Narrows. Verrazzano took a small boat to explore and entered New York Bay. He assumed it was a large lake. If he had kept going, Verrazzano may have found the Hudson River. However, strong winds forced him back to his ship.

JUST LIKE HOME!

+ Mediterranean scenery

After leaving New York Bay, *La Dauphine* turned north along the coast of Long Island. As he passed Block Island (right), Verrazzano thought it looked like the island of Rhodes, in Greece. He noted the beauty of the land and named it Louisa, for the mother of King Francis. The weather was bad, so Verrazzano kept heading north and landed in what is now Newport Harbor, Rhode Island. The crew spent 15 days exploring the area.

AN AMERICAN CAPE

☛ **Sailing past**

In 1529, Verrazzano's brother, the mapmaker Girolamo Verrazzano, drew a map of the world that included the American coast. He charted the unusual shape of Cape Cod (left). France later founded its **colonies** to the north. This area came under English control in the 1600s. The Pilgrims from England arrived at Plymouth Rock, Cape Cod, in 1620.

GIOVANNI DA VERRAZZANO'S VOYAGE TO NORTH AMERICA

The precise locations visited by Verrazzano as he sailed up the east coast of North America are not known, but historians believe they have identified his probable route and the places he visited.

Key

•••••► 1524 voyage

Modern national borders

Locator map

UNITED STATES

Cape Fear

This headland in North Carolina was the first place Verrazzano reached in North America after a 50-day voyage. He described seeing fires lit by Native peoples all along the shore.

Maine

Verrazzano was impressed by the vast forests he saw in Maine. Forests were vitally important at a time when wood was the main material for constructing both buildings and ships. However, the local Penobscot people were hostile to the Europeans.

Narragansett Bay

This **estuary** in what is now Rhode Island was home to the Narragansett and Wampanoag peoples. It was the area where Verrazzano spent the most time.

Cape Cod

Verrazzano sailed past Cape Cod, which has a distinctive fishhook shape, but dangerous patches of rocks prevented him from landing. The region later became a center of English colonization.

CANADA

Newfoundland

Maine

Long Island

N
NW
NE
W
E
SW
SE
S

310 miles
Scale ⊢————————————⊣
500 km

New York Bay

As he sailed up the coast, Verrazzano sailed into a large bay, where he met the Lenape people. This was probably what is now New York Harbor. If he continued, he might have discovered the Hudson River, but strong winds forced him to turn back.

Outer Banks

Verrazzano mistook this string of sand islands for the extent of the whole American continent. He believed the water he could see beyond the islands was the Pacific Ocean—in fact, it was Pamlico Sound.

Meet the Crew

Verrazzano sailed at a time when many Europeans were interested in exploring North America. They hoped to make money through trade.

Brother

Verrazzano's brother, Girolamo, mapped the American coast. In 1529, Girolamo drew a world map for Pope Clement VII. It showed the coastline accurately but depicted North America as a strip of land between the Atlantic and Pacific oceans.

SHIP OWNER

+ Dieppe businessman sponsors voyages

Jean Ango inherited his father's shipping business in Dieppe, France. He became wealthy and eventually owned about 70 ships. Ango was famous for his **humanist** views and was a close advisor to King Francis I. Ango supplied vessels for the king's explorers, including supplying *La Dauphine* for Verrazzano's 1524 voyage. In addition to his interest in exploration, Ango was involved in **piracy**. His ships' captains seized treasures from Spanish and Portuguese vessels.

ROYAL CONNECTIONS

☛ **Ambitions abroad**

☛ **Competing with Spain**

Francis I (right) became king of France in 1515. Francis developed a fierce rivalry with Charles I of Spain. By the 1520s, the Spanish had claimed parts of southern North America and South America. Francis I was determined to expand France's territory and wealth by finding a route to East Asia, which was the source of valuable trade goods. Francis wanted Verrazzano to look for a route to the north of the Spanish territories in America. If Verrazzano could find the route to Asia, France would have an advantage over Spain and the rest of Europe.

" Now on our return from this voyage, I will tell Your Majesty of what we found." *Verrazzano in a letter to King Francis I from Dieppe, July 1524.*

GREAT AMBITION

☛ French admiral hungry for power

Philippe de Chabot was a childhood friend of Francis I. He remained close to the king and became an admiral in the French navy. Chabot rose in power and wealth. By 1527, he was able to help sponsor Verrazzano's voyage to Brazil. He later also helped sponsor Jacques Cartier's expedition to what is now Canada in 1534.

AROUND THE WORLD

+ Stimulates more exploration

Born in Portugal, Ferdinand Magellan (above) explored on behalf of Spain. In 1519, he set out with a fleet of five ships and sailed around the tip of South America and across the Pacific Ocean. Magellan died in the Philippines, but his remaining crew returned to Spain in 1522. This was the first **circumnavigation** of the globe. Reports of the voyage created great excitement in Europe. French merchants were convinced that a quicker route to East Asia could be found by sailing west. They urged Francis I to **sponsor** Verrazzano to find it.

Check Out the Ride

In the 1500s, Europeans built great sailing ships for ocean voyages. Caravels and carracks became the standard vessels for trade, warfare, and exploration, leading to the discovery of the New World.

LA DAUPHINE

+ Vessels secured for first journey

+ Ship bears royal name

Verrazzano began his 1524 expedition with four ships, but only one made the journey across the Atlantic. *La Dauphine* was a **carrack** (right), built in 1518. It had three masts. The main mast and foremast had square sails. The third, or mizzenmast, had a triangular sail. Carracks had high **forecastles** and **aftercastles** to house cabins for the sailors. The ships were used for trade, but they also carried cannons for defense. European **shipwrights** developed the vessels specifically for long-distance ocean trade.

ALL ABOARD!

☛ Verrazzano assembles his crew

Like other carracks (left), *La Dauphine* was wide and deep. The ship carried 50 men, plus enough food and supplies to last eight months. Most of the men would have been poor working sailors. Verrazzano's record of the voyage only mentions two names: his brother, Girolamo, and Antoine de Conflans, the ship's pilot.

SHIP SET TO SAIL AGAIN

★ **Museum honors historic ship**

★ **Anniversary voyage planned**

The Maritime Museum in Rouen, France, holds a scale **replica** of *La Dauphine*. The museum is also building a full-size version of the ship. The builders hope to complete the project and sail the ship to New York in 2024 to mark the 500th anniversary of Verrazzano's historic voyage.

 Weather Forecast

ANGRY OCEAN

The Atlantic Ocean experiences a variety of weather. Verrazzano and his crew had to be ready for many conditions, including fierce storms with harsh winds and rain, or wintry weather in the North Atlantic. Farther south, their ships sometimes got stuck for days in regions of little wind and baking sun.

TRAVEL UPDATE

Learning From the Locals!

★ If you're visiting a new place, try learning from the people who live there. Verrazzano met Native peoples who used dugout canoes to travel by water. The canoes were large and sturdy, and could carry up to 12 people. They were made from cedar or pine trees. Fire and stone tools were used to hollow out the tree trunk (above). The process could take many days.

Did you know ?

Verrazzano's ship, *La Dauphine*, was named in honor of the heir to the throne in France, known as the dauphin. *Dauphine* means "dolphin," and refers to the animal on the family crest.

Solve It With Science

Giovanni and Girolamo da Verrazzano would have used the latest European technology to help them find their way across the Atlantic Ocean.

IT'S IN THE STARS

★ Night sky leads the way

★ Instruments help measure positions

Explorers in the early 1500s had a number of **navigation** instruments to help them. Verrazzano probably used an astrolabe (below). This device measures the angle between the **horizon** and Polaris, or the North Star. Verrazzano could read the degrees marked on the edge of the astrolabe and calculate the ship's **latitude**, or north–south position. Verrazzano may have used a wooden cross staff to measure the height of the Sun or the North Star above the horizon. The angle formed the basis for figuring latitude.

SURVEYING THE LAND

☛ Charting the coastline

☛ Mistakes along the way

As *La Dauphine* followed the coastline, Verrazzano made notes. He compared the landforms and the latitude with places he knew in Europe. However, he preferred not to sail too close to the shore, so he missed features such as the Hudson River and the Bay of Fundy. He mistakenly claimed that Pamlico Sound was part of a large sea leading to the Pacific Ocean. For over a century, mapmakers included the Verrazzano Sea on maps (as at the top center of the map above).

WIDE, WIDE WORLD

+ Earth's size estimated

As he sailed, Verrazzano calculated the distance he traveled and noted his latitude in a logbook. The logbook was lost, but Verrazzano made many references to his observations in the letter he wrote to Francis I in July 1524. Verrazzano used the observations to calculate that the Earth was 18,759 miles (30,190 km) around. Despite the explorer's math skills, he was not quite right. In fact, the Earth's **circumference** is 24,874 miles (40,030 km).

My Explorer Journal

★ **Imagine you are a sailor on** *La Dauphine*. **Using details in this book, write your own logbook entry. Describe the weather conditions and give details of some of the places that Verrazzano visited.**

BEARING GIFTS

☛ Tools and mirrors fail to impress

Verrazzano carried guns to scare any hostile peoples he met, plus metal tools (below) and mirrors to trade. Verrazzano describes firing a gun only once. He said that it made a local man "tremble with fear." When the Europeans tried trading with the Narragansett, the tribe did not think much of European goods. They refused to take silk and laughed at the mirrors. They were only interested in small bells and jewelry.

DEAD RECKONING

★ Navigating the old way

Verrazzano likely learned dead reckoning from older mariners. This form of navigation estimated a ship's location. A sailor calculated the direction and speed of the ship and the time it spent sailing. That gave a sense of how far the ship had traveled. The method was basic but useful, especially during the day, when navigators could not navigate by the stars (above left).

Hanging at Home

For most of the expedition, Verrazzano and his crew were cooped up on *La Dauphine*. However, in the little time they spent ashore, they glimpsed Native ways of life.

COMFORTS OF HOME

- ☞ Tribal living
- ☞ Moving with the seasons

In Narragansett Bay, Verrazzano observed the local people and how they lived. The traditional home was a circular wigwam (above). The Narragansett constructed these homes with **saplings** covered with layers of straw. They used these homes for the spring and summer farming season. In the winter, they moved to warmer homes inland.

OFFICERS VS. CREW

+ Trouble onboard

Verrazzano does not seem to have gotten along with his crew. He called them "la turba maritima"—a **maritime** mob. The crew likely found Verrazzano difficult, too. He did not allow them to go ashore for long. He seems to have taken them for granted and never calls any of them by name. In his letter to the king, Verrazzano gives his ship credit for surviving the voyage but only mentions his men in passing.

COASTAL LIVING
★ Living well

The Narragansett lived according to the seasons. In spring and summer, they farmed squash, corn, and beans near the coast. The ocean was a rich source of cod, flatfish, and other seafood. Women gathered clams (left) and crabs on the shore and picked nuts and berries in the woods. In winter, the men hunted beaver, deer, and other animals. Other coastal peoples, such as the Penobscot, did not farm. They depended on hunting, fishing, and gathering wild roots.

 Weather Forecast

STORM APPROACHING!

La Dauphine survived its first storm in January 1524 and endured more violent weather in the western Atlantic Ocean. Carracks were heavy ships with high sides that helped keep them steady. The three masts meant that carracks sailed better in strong winds.

TRAVEL UPDATE

What's for Dinner?

★ If you're planning a long sea voyage, make sure to take enough fresh fruit. *La Dauphine* carried dried fish and meat, **hardtack**, beer, and wine, but little fresh food. Without fresh fruit and vegetables, sailors fell ill from **scurvy**. Verrazzano and his men did not have wilderness survival skills, so they could not hunt for fresh food. When their supplies ran low near Newfoundland, Verrazzano decided to head back to France.

Meeting and Greeting

Verrazzano spent little time ashore in America, but during his short stays on land, he was an eager observer of the local people's appearance and behavior.

Kidnapped!

North of Pamlico Sound, Verrazzano and his men went ashore. They seized a young Native boy and took him to their ship. No one knows what happened to the boy after he was taken to France.

SIGNS OF LIFE

☞ Campfires light the shore

As Verrazzano sailed along the coast, he saw campfires all along the shore. The Native peoples who made the fires may have been Waccamaw or Tuscarora (right). Farther north were the Nanticoke, the Powhatan **Confederacy**, the Wampanoag, the Narragansett, and the Penobscot. Many more tribes made their homes inland. Scholars estimate that millions of people lived in North America before Europeans arrived. Contact with Europeans devastated these peoples through disease, warfare, and loss of their tribal lands.

A HELPING HAND

★ Injured sailor tended on shore

★ Local people mean no harm

North of Cape Fear, Verrazzano sent 25 men ashore on a small boat to find fresh water. High waves made it impossible for the boat to land, so a young sailor tried to swim ashore. He almost drowned. When he washed up on the beach, local people rushed to help him. They carried him to safety and made a fire to keep him warm. When the sailor was well enough, he returned to the ship.

MAKING FRIENDS

+ First meetings in the New World

+ Europeans offer gifts

Verrazzano and his crew were the first Europeans many Native peoples had seen. Some, such as the Cape Fear people, were initially frightened. The Narragansett were more confident, but the men made sure to keep the women away from the Europeans and their ship. All but the Penobscot were generous and friendly. Most tribal people gave the Europeans food and allowed them to see their homes (left). In return, Verrazzano offered them small gifts such as fishing hooks and other metal objects.

> They live for a long time, and rarely fall sick. If they fall sick, they cure themselves with fire without medicine."
> *Verrazzano describes Native people.*

TRAVEL UPDATE

Listen Carefully!

★ One way to learn about people that you meet when traveling is to study their languages. The Algonquians lived in North Carolina and farther north. They belonged to the Algonquin language group. Explorers, such as Verrazzano, did not notice differences between tribes. However, each Algonquian group, such as the Pamlico, Secotan, and Croatan, spoke a separate **dialect**. They had their own dress (right), communities, and chiefs.

People of the Northeast

Many of the Native peoples Verrazzano met were generous and kind to the visitors. However, a few tribes sensed danger, and were hostile to the Europeans.

Errors

Verrazzano often misunderstood Native peoples. For example, he assumed they did not have any religion. In fact, most peoples had a complex system of gods and myths.

TIDEWATER PEOPLE
☞ Coastal farmers

The boy Verrazzano kidnapped may have belonged to a small tribe called the Nanticoke. The Nanticoke lived in Delaware and Maryland. Their name comes from a word meaning "tidewater people." The Nanticoke were farmers who grew squash, beans, corn, pumpkin, and other crops. The men used spears and nets to fish in the rivers and ocean. After Verrazzano's visit, the Nanticoke did not meet any other Europeans until English settlers came to the area in 1608.

THE GRANDFATHERS
★ Lenape greet their visitors
★ Friendly relations

The Lenni Lenape are one of the oldest tribes of the Northeast. Other peoples call them the "grandfathers." Before Europeans settled in North America, many thousands of Lenape lived in villages in present-day New Jersey, New York, Delaware, and Pennsylvania. According to Verrazzano, the Lenape wore colorful birds' feathers. The Lenape greeted the Europeans warmly and showed them a safe place to put their boat. They also showed the visitors around their villages (right).

A ROYAL WELCOME

- ☛ Tribal chiefs go aboard *La Dauphine*
- ☛ Gifts and food exchanged

On Rhode Island, Verrazzano likely met the Narragansett. In the 1500s, they numbered at least 10,000 people in eight major communities. The chiefs and the women wore embroidered deerskin clothing and necklaces of colored stones. The Narragansett impressed Verrazzano with their appearance and manners.

Did you know ?

The Penobscot may have met Europeans before Verrazzano arrived. French fishermen had sailed to the area. These early meetings may have caused the tribe to be cautious when they met Verrazzano.

YOU'RE NOT INVITED!

+ A hostile welcome

In the 1500s, the tribes of the Western and Eastern Abenaki included about 25,000 people. They lived across a large area, including Maine. Verrazzano probably met the Penobscot people, members of the Eastern Abenaki. The Penobscot were expert hunters (above) and fishers. Verrazzano noticed their clothes made from bear, lynx, and other animal skins. He called them "**barbarous**." The Penobscot were suspicious of the Europeans. In order to trade with them, they sent their goods on a rope in exchange for knives and metal objects.

I Love Nature

Verrazzano had his first glimpse of North America in early spring 1524. He was amazed at the rich and varied landscape and the range of plants he saw.

Vikings

The earliest Viking explorers arrived in North America around 1000 CE. They probably landed in what is now Newfoundland. They named the area Vinland for the many vines they found growing there.

A GLOWING REPORT

+ Beauty all around

Verrazzano did not find a route to East Asia, but he did not want to disappoint Francis I. In his letter to the king, the explorer described the great opportunities for French settlement in North America. He named the land Francesca, in honor of Francis. Verrazzano was full of admiration for this new land. He compared its landscape to beautiful parts of Europe such as Greece and Italy (above). Although Verrazzano did not inspect the land closely, he claimed that the ground was full of **minerals**, including gold.

BRILLIANT BLOOMS

★ **Flowers catch Verrazzano's eye**

★ **Scents reach the ship**

The countryside was full of wild flowers in spring. Verrazzano recognized lilies, violets, and wild roses, but many other flowers were new to the Europeans. He may have seen white trilliums, wild ginger, or Virginia bluebells (right). All of these are native to the northeastern United States.

REMINDERS OF HOME

- ☞ Climbing vines spark interest
- ☞ Local farming methods

As the expedition sailed past Delaware and New Jersey, Verrazzano noticed many vines climbing up the trees. He compared them to grapevines that grew in Italy. Verrazzano pointed out to the king that the French could try winemaking in the New World. He also recorded how the local people, possibly the Lenape, tended their vines (right). They cleared the land to allow more fruit to grow. The Lenape and other tribes used controlled fires to clear the land. This method of **cultivation** ensured that the land stayed fertile.

Did you know ?

Verrazzano reported that the soil was so rich that "any kind of seed would produce excellent crops." Many Native peoples he met were farmers. They moved and planted as the seasons changed.

 Weather Forecast

NOTHING BUT BLUE SKIES!

Verrazzano found the climate in North Carolina pleasant. He said that the sky was "clear and cloudless, with infrequent rain." He was surprised that Rhode Island was cooler, because he calculated that its latitude was the same as Rome, Italy. Verrazzano suggested that the air was not usually so cool.

NEW WORLD FORESTS

★ A world of trees

Verrazzano noted lush forests from North Carolina to Maine (left). He identified many different types of trees. There were laurels, palms, and cypresses in the south. The scent from the trees was so strong that he could smell it from his ship. Farther north, he spotted oaks as well as apple and plum trees.

Fortune Hunting

French traders were eager to increase their wealth. They paid for Verrazzano's voyages in the hope of finding resources, such as fish or wood, or of opening new trade routes.

TRAVEL UPDATE

Reports of a Fantastic Discovery

★ One way to get people to believe the stories of your travels is to exaggerate a little. Although Verrazzano did not reach East Asia, he believed Pamlico Sound would lead to Cathay, or China (right). To make this seem more likely, Verrazzano made many references to East Asia when describing the region. He wrote that the people had "oriental" features and that the air was fragrant with spices.

GET RICH QUICK!

★ **Explorer seeks new trade route**

★ **Northwest Passage sought**

In the 1500s, Europeans believed an easy westward sea route existed to East Asia. They called it the Northwest Passage. At the time, no one realized how huge North America was. European explorers continued to look for the Northwest Passage for 300 years. Although a route through the Arctic was eventually found in the early 1900s, ice made it too difficult to be useful for trade.

★ **Imagine you are Verrazzano and the Portuguese catch you smuggling brazilwood. Using information from this book, write a letter to King Francis asking him to step in and speak to the Portuguese on your behalf.**

MISSED CHANCE
☞ France lets opportunity go

Verrazzano claimed all the land he explored on behalf of France, but Francis I decided not to send Verrazzano back to the region. Instead, the French explorer Jacques Cartier led an expedition in 1534 to explore Newfoundland and the St. Lawrence River. Cartier claimed what is now Canada and named it New France (above left). Later, the French set up short-lived colonies in South Carolina and Florida. Farther north, Britain, Holland, and Sweden settled the coast that Verrazzano had explored.

Compliment

Verrazzano gave different names to different places he found, but he named the whole land "Francesca," in honor of King Francis. He probably wanted to flatter the French king.

ILLEGAL CARGO
★ **Bankers want wood for France**
★ **Smuggling voyage planned**

Brazilwood from Brazil (right) was highly prized in Europe. The wood was good for construction, but more importantly the sawdust could be soaked in water to create a valuable red dye. The Portuguese claimed Brazil and controlled the brazilwood trade. Pirates from other countries seized brazilwood from Portuguese ships as they crossed the Atlantic. When Verrazzano visited Brazil in 1526, he smuggled out illegal brazilwood.

This Isn't What It Said in the Brochure!

Things do not always go as planned. Verrazzano's journeys began and ended with trouble. Severe storms and hostile tribes caused destruction and death.

Did you know ?

Europeans could only communicate with Native peoples by using hand gestures and signals. This caused confusion, and sometimes led to misunderstandings and violence.

STORM DAMAGE

☛ Shipwreck causes delay

☛ Solo ship braves the ocean waves

When Verrazzano left France in late 1523, he planned to lead four ships across the Atlantic Ocean. He did not get far. Fierce winds and high waves sank two ships, and the battered *Normande* and *La Dauphine* returned to France. After repairing the ships, Verrazzano set out again. This time, King Francis recalled the *Normande* to fight against Spain. In the end, Verrazzano finally set sail with only *La Dauphine*. He left Madeira, in Spain, on January 17, 1524.

 Weather Forecast

DANGEROUS SEAS!

After *La Dauphine* had been sailing for 25 days across the Atlantic, it was caught in a storm that lasted 16 hours. Verrazzano called it "a storm as violent as ever sailing man encountered." He said that he and his crew only survived with divine help—and because *La Dauphine* was so sturdy.

IT'S CROWDED IN HERE

- ☛ Cramped quarters spark arguments
- ☛ Too close for comfort

Ocean travel in the 1500s was not comfortable. As captain, Verrazzano probably slept in his own small cabin. Some crew may have had hammocks (below right), but most slept on the floor or on the ship's deck. Sailing a carrack was a full-time job. The crew would take shifts throughout the day. Young boys scrubbed the deck while more experienced crew worked the sails. Such difficult living conditions caused problems. Men argued, food was scarce, and Verrazzano was not a sympathetic captain.

> " Since we had exhausted all our naval stores and provisions, we decided to return to France."
> *Verrazzano describes the end of the voyage.*

My Explorer Journal

★ **Verrazzano's meeting with the Penobscot people was unsuccessful. Do you think he could have done anything differently? Write down your ideas.**

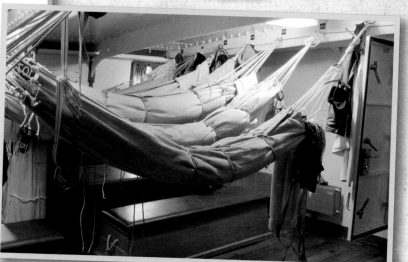

UNDER ATTACK

★ **Arrows shot at Verrazzano**

★ **No friends here**

Verrazzano did not like the Penobscot he met in Maine. He found them "full of crudity and vices." The Penobscot would only trade at a distance. They exchanged food and furs for the fishhooks and knives offered by the Europeans. Even so, Verrazzano and 25 of his men ventured ashore. He claimed to have visited Penobscot homes, though this seems unlikely. As the Europeans approached the shore in their boat, tribal warriors shot arrows at them (left).

End of the Road

After Verrazzano's death, other people went on to claim the territory he had explored. However, he had greatly increased European knowledge of the Americas.

Forgotten

After his death, Verrazzano was almost completely forgotten. His letter describing his voyage was dismissed as a fake. Opinions about him only changed in the 1900s.

SAILING TO BRAZIL

☞ Another expedition for Verrazzano

La Dauphine returned to France from North America in July, 1524. Verrazzano was eager to return to exploring, but French bankers were not interested in his New World. They arranged for Verrazzano to take four ships to Brazil to harvest brazilwood. Verrazzano set off with four ships in 1527. A storm forced one ship off course. The other three sailed to Brazil, and Verrazzano loaded them with the valuable wood.

FINAL JOURNEY

★ A violent end

★ Brother watches in horror

Verrazzano set sail on his last journey in 1528. This time, he sailed into Spanish territory in Florida and the Caribbean. Again, Verrazzano was hoping to find a route to Asia. According to an account written in Italy 20 years later, Verrazzano and Girolamo rowed ashore at Guadeloupe. A group of people waited, possibly from the Carib tribe (right). Verrazzano went forward and the Carib attacked him. Without a gun, Girolamo could not protect his brother. The Caribs killed Verrazzano and ate his remains.

EXPLORERS

+ Other names become famous

After Verrazzano died, his achievements were largely forgotten. The French sent Jacques Cartier and later, Samuel de Champlain to explore parts of what is now Canada. Meanwhile, other explorers, such as the Englishman Henry Hudson, ventured further inland than Verrazzano. Hudson's explorations, including sailing up the Hudson River (right), became much better known than those of Verrazzano.

ALTERNATIVE ENDING

★ **Doubt surrounds explorer's death**

★ **Dishonor for Verrazzano?**

Most scholars accept that Verrazzano died in the Caribbean. However, no proof exists. This has created different ideas about the explorer's final days. One idea is that the Spanish arrested and killed Verrazzano for piracy after he sailed into Spanish territory and stole brazilwood for France.

LASTING MONUMENTS

☛ **Bridges recognize achievements**

Two bridges in the United States honor Verrazzano and his explorations. The Verrazano–Narrows Bridge (left) links Brooklyn and Staten Island in New York State. The bridge, which opened in 1964, crosses the **strait** called the Verrazano Narrows. Two other bridges bear the explorer's name. In Maryland, the Verrazano Bridge crosses Sinepuxent Bay. In Rhode Island, the Jamestown–Verrazano Bridge connects Jamestown with North Kingstown. Opened in 1992, this bridge honors the area where Verrazzano spent the most time on land.

GLOSSARY

aftercastles Raised structures at the back, or stern, of a ship

barbarous Uncultured and unpleasant

carrack A large ocean-going sailing ship

circumference The distance around the outside of a circle or sphere

circumnavigation A voyage all the way around the world

circumstantial Evidence that suggests something but does not prove it

colonies Areas in one country settled and controlled by people from another country

confederacy A group of peoples joined together for a common purpose

cultivation Planting and raising crops

dialect A local variation of a language

divine Related to a god

estuary The mouth where a large river meets the sea

forecastles Raised structures at the front of a ship

hardtack A flat, hard, unsalted cracker that did not rot during long voyages

headland A narrow piece of land that sticks into the sea

horizon The line at which the ground or sea seems to meet the sky

humanist Someone who believes life is based on reason and science rather than superstition

latitude The position of a location north or south of the equator

maritime Related to the sea

minerals A solid, naturally occuring substance that does not come from plants or animals

navigation Planning and following a route, and identifying one's location

piracy Attacking and stealing from ships at sea

replica An exact copy or model of something

saplings Young trees

scurvy A deadly disease caused by a lack of Vitamin C

shipwrights Craftspeople who build ships

sound A large saltwater inlet, or body of water, between two bodies of land

sponsor To pay the costs of something

strait A narrow passage of water connecting two large bodies of water

tidewater Describes a region that is affected by the ocean tides

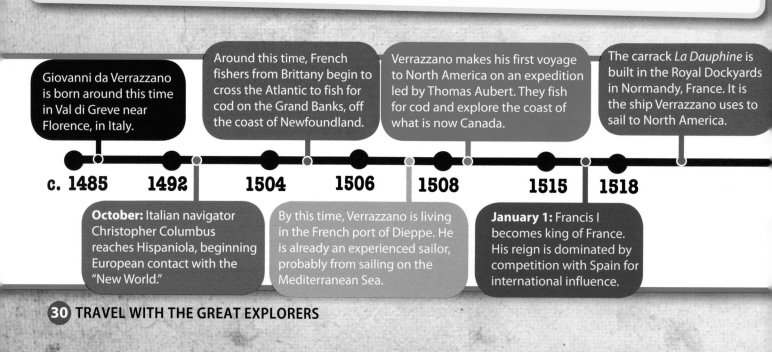

Giovanni da Verrazzano is born around this time in Val di Greve near Florence, in Italy.

Around this time, French fishers from Brittany begin to cross the Atlantic to fish for cod on the Grand Banks, off the coast of Newfoundland.

Verrazzano makes his first voyage to North America on an expedition led by Thomas Aubert. They fish for cod and explore the coast of what is now Canada.

The carrack *La Dauphine* is built in the Royal Dockyards in Normandy, France. It is the ship Verrazzano uses to sail to North America.

c. 1485   1492   1504   1506   1508   1515   1518

October: Italian navigator Christopher Columbus reaches Hispaniola, beginning European contact with the "New World."

By this time, Verrazzano is living in the French port of Dieppe. He is already an experienced sailor, probably from sailing on the Mediterranean Sea.

January 1: Francis I becomes king of France. His reign is dominated by competition with Spain for international influence.

ON THE WEB

nationalhumanitiescenter.org/pds/
amerbegin/contact/text4/
verrazzano.pdf
An edited, illustrated version of Verrazzano's letter to the king.

ageofex.marinersmuseum.org/index.
php?type=explorer&id=22
A biography of Verrazzano from the Mariners' Museum.

www1.musee-maritime-rouen.asso.
fr/restauration-navale/la-dauphine/
A page from the Maritime Museum in Rouen about building the replica version of *La Dauphine* (the page is in French, but has a "translate" button).

exploration.marinersmuseum.org/
subject/giovanni-da-verrazzano/
Interesting facts about Verrazzano, with a map.

www.timetoast.com/timelines/
giovanni-da-verrazzano--8
A brief timeline of Verrazzano's life.

BOOKS

Cosson, M. J. *America: Three Worlds Meet: Beginnings to 1620* (History Digs). Cherry Lake Publishing, 2011.

Elliott, Lynne. *Exploration in the Renaissance* (Renaissance World). Crabtree Publishing Company, 2009.

Gitlin, Marty. *Giovanni da Verrazzano* (Spotlight on Explorers and Colonization). Rosen Young Adult, 2016.

Sonneborn, Liz. *Native Peoples of the Northeast* (North American Indian Nations). Lerner Publications, 2016.

September 6: The survivors of Ferdinand Magellan's expedition around the world return to Spain. The successful circumnavigation stimulates new efforts at exploration in France.

January 17: Verrazzano sets out from Madeira onboard *La Dauphine*.

July 7: Around this time, Verrazzano returns to Dieppe and writes to King Francis describing his voyage.

On a voyage to the Caribbean, Verrazzano is probably killed by Native peoples in Guadeloupe.

1522   **1523**   **1524**   **1527**   **1528**

Francis I asks Verrazzano to look for a route to the Pacific Ocean on behalf of France.

Late in the year, Verrazzano sets out across the Atlantic with four ships, but bad weather forces him to turn back.

March: Verrazzano makes landfall near what is now Cape Fear, North Carolina. He begins sailing north along the coast.

Verrazzano sails with three ships to Brazil in order to seize an illegal cargo of brazilwood.

INDEX